Inventions That Shaped the World

THE CLOCK

WIL MARA

Franklin Watts
A Division of Scholastic Inc.
New York · Toronto · London · Auckland · Sydney
Mexico City · New Delhi · Hong Kong
Danbury, Connecticut

Photographs © 2005: Art Resource, NY: 24 (Jost Burgi/Bridgeman-Giraudon), 16 (Victoria & Albert Museum, London); Corbis Images: 48 (Lester V. Bergman), cover, 23 (Bettmann), 18 (Philip de Bay/Historical Picture Archive), cover background (First Light), 63 (Hulton-Deutsch Collection), 21 (Matthias Kulka), 14 (Kevin R. Morris), 58 (Rob & Sas), chapter openers, 54, 60 (Royalty-Free), 34 (Paul A. Souders), 66 (Eriko Sugita/X00273/Reuters), 22, 35; Fundamental Photos, New York: 57 (Diane Hirsch), 40 (Jack Plekan); Getty Images/Ben Martin/Time Life Pictures: 64; Mary Evans Picture Library: 62 (C. H. Lane), 8 (Poyet); North Wind Picture Archives: 13, 61; Photo Researchers, NY: 29, 45 (SPL), 27 (Sheila Terry/SPL); Photri Inc.: 69 (M. Gibson), 46, 51, 55; The Art Archive/Picture Desk/Dagli Orti: 12 (Marine Museum Lisbon), 15 (Museo Naval Madrid), 25 (Observatory Academy Florence Italy); The Image Works: 52 (Rob Crandall), 10 (HIP/Ann Ronan Picture Library), 19 (HIP/University of York), 50 (Johannes Kroemer/Visum), 6 (Dion Ogust), chapter openers, 26, 31, 32, 36, 38, 39, 65 (SSPL), 28, 44, 70, 71 (SSPL/Science Museum), 17 (Charles Walker/Topfoto).

Cover design by The Design Lab
Book production by The Design Lab

Library of Congress Cataloging-in-Publication Data

Mara, Wil.
 The clock / by Wil Mara.
   p. cm. — (Inventions that shaped the world)
 Includes bibliographical references and index.
 ISBN 0-531-12373-1 (lib. bdg.)   0-531-16743-7 (pbk.)
 1. Clocks and watches—Juvenile literature. I. Title. II. Series.
 TS542.5.M37 2005
 681.1'13—dc22   2004030270

CONTENTS

Time to Talk About Time

Take a look at a nearby *clock.* It may be hanging on a wall, sitting on a shelf, or wrapped around your wrist. What time is it?

Now imagine a world without clocks. There are no numbers marking off the hours, minutes, and seconds. You have no idea when your favorite TV show will be on, when you need to get out of bed, or when to call one of your friends. It's all guesswork. The closest thing to a time-keeping device is the sun. When the sun is directly over your head, it's noon, or close to it. But even the sun can be misleading because it rises and sets at different times depending on the season and where you live on the planet.

We live in an age when clocks are a normal part of our routine. They structure everything we do. Whether you're five or eighty-five, you rely on clocks dozens of times a day. It's almost impossible to imagine a world without them. The moment we wake up, we check a clock. We build our days around schedules, and we get nervous if we are running late. Time is the most precious commodity we have. The richest person in the world can't buy more of it.

Through the years, humans have grown increasingly obsessed with the concept of time. The history of *horology* (the science of measuring time) tells the tale of the men and women who struggled to find ways to measure time with ever-greater accuracy.

A girl punches a time clock to start her work day.

THE NEED TO KNOW

Think about what the world was like tens of thousands of years ago. There were no cars, no buildings, no telephones, and no computers. Every person had just one priority—survival. People didn't worry about retrieving the messages on the answering machine or setting the timer on the VCR. They were too busy building shelters and hunting food. They lived in caves or huts and drank from streams and rivers. They could perform important chores only during daylight hours. Night was for resting. There was no reason to care what time it was.

Then, about five thousand years ago, people started wanting to tell time more accurately. Their early attempts at timekeeping were crude and inaccurate. The *obelisk,* a narrow stone column that cast shadows on the ground to

This Chinese clepsydra, or water clock, from the fourteenth century was one early kind of clock.

mark the movement of the sun, was crude and inaccurate. The *sundial* and the *water clock,* or clepsydra, were other early attempts at timekeeping.

Early Mechanical Clocks

No one knows who invented the first *mechanical clock.* Some historians think they were first developed in Europe between 1200 and 1300. Others say there is evidence that they were created in China before 1200. Blacksmiths were probably involved in the creation of these first clocks because of the complexity of the metalwork involved. At this time, the habit of dividing each day into two large sections of twelve hours each began to evolve into the twenty-four hour-long divisions we still use today.

There are some facts we do know about the earliest mechanical clocks. They had no dials, no numbers, and no hands. They ran on a set of interconnected gears and were often powered by a slow-falling weight of some kind—a stone, for example—attached to the end of a string or chain. In short, the earliest mechanical clocks were very simple machines that looked nothing like the clocks we know today.

Humans have always been *diurnal.* Our biological nature is to do most of our work during the day, then rest at night. As our desire to become more productive increased, so did our desire to organize our time. The birth of the mechanical clock began to change the way we viewed time. It was a significant moment in human history. You probably know, with fair accuracy, what time you woke up today, took a shower, ate breakfast, and so on. You probably also know what time you're expected to be home at night and what time your favorite TV shows come on. A thousand years ago, people didn't have these concerns. They had no need for this kind of "time sensitivity."

In the late thirteenth century, however, monks in Europe sought greater precision in the existing mechanical clocks. They wanted to live more disciplined, structured lives. They experimented with time-keeping devices that automatically rang bells at certain hours. This allowed them to pray, do their chores, eat their meals, offer religious guidance to others, and sleep on a set schedule. The improvements they made to the accuracy of early clocks helped provide more accurate clocks for the rest of the world.

Ancient astronomers, such as Hipparchus (above), tracked the movements of the stars. Astronomers needed clocks to do their work and challenged inventors to come up with more accurate clocks.

Early astronomers were also a driving force behind increasing the accuracy of timekeeping. They followed the paths of stars in the night sky and tracked them with the help of clocks. Combined with some basic mathematical formulas, they could roughly determine a star's proximity to Earth or to other stars simply by timing its movement. These astronomers had little use for clocks that couldn't divide time into precise units such as minutes or seconds. They challenged craftspeople to create the most accurate clocks of their era. These advances also occurred during the 1300s.

Sailor's Delight

Sailors were also in great need of accurate clocks. In the earliest explorations of the world's vast waterways, it was impossible to tell how far east or west a ship was traveling. Tracking distances north or south was relatively simple if a sailor knew how to calculate the position of the sun or the stars and he brought along a reliable compass.

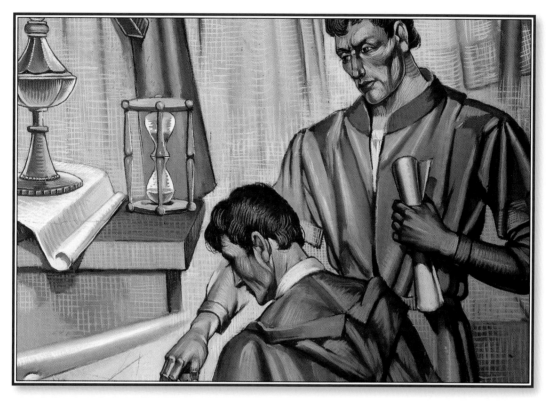

Prince Henry the Navigator's cartographers, or mapmakers, work on a map. To navigate safely, a ship's captain needs a reliable clock that tells the time at a known longitudinal position.

Judging distances east or west, however, was more difficult. Each ship required a clock that kept precise time. Here's why.

Imagine Earth turning slowly in space. Divide the Earth into 360 even parts. Now imagine the boundaries of those parts as lines, 360 of them running north to south, called lines of longitude. Earth makes one full rotation in twenty-four hours. Divide those 360 lines by 24 and you get 15—each line is 15 degrees from the other. So, 15 degrees of longitude equals one hour of reliable time, but not necessarily one hour's duration in travel, especially at the poles.

Knowing this, a ship's captain had to bring along a reliable clock that told the time at a known longitudinal position. For example, if a ship was docked at a port positioned at 35 degrees longitude, the captain might set sail at noon, or the time at which the sun was directly overhead. He would also set his clock to this time. Then,

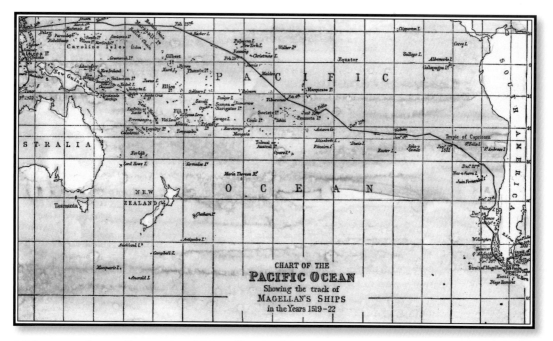

This map shows the route of Magellan's ships across the Pacific during their circumnavigation of Earth in 1519–1522. These early voyages of discovery were dangerous and could be deadly if the ship's captain didn't have a reliable clock to help him determine the ship's position.

once at sea, he would always know what time it was back at that position. Using this information, all he had to do was wait for high noon on the ocean to determine the time difference between the home port and his current position. But if the clock he brought along wasn't completely reliable, it was useless. It was also dangerous. A ship that lost its way often steered into storms, landed on unfriendly shores, or ran out of supplies.

Knowing the Time While at Sea—A Tragic Story

A particularly horrible accident inspired the modern search for a reliable sea clock. In October 1707, more than two thousand British sailors drowned off the southwestern coast of England after they incorrectly calculated their longitude and crashed into the rocks of the Scilly Isles. As a result, the British Parliament passed the Longitude Act in July 1714, which offered a huge cash prize to anyone who could design a clock that provided reliable time at sea.

An hourglass is a simple device to measure one hour of time. Just turn the hourglass over and let the sand fall to the bottom. When all the sand falls, one hour has passed.

Many early mechanical clocks were works of art that people kept as signs of their wealth.

Looking Good

In the days of the earliest mechanical clocks, many people kept them as a sign of stature and prosperity. Hundreds of years ago, people paid huge amounts of money just for the prestige of owning a clock. The same was true for towns—there was no greater sign of a community's affluence than having a clock tower in the town square. It didn't matter that these clocks often couldn't maintain the correct time. They were usually beautifully crafted and decorated works of art. But today, you can find inexpensive clocks and watches in supermarkets, drugstore, and many other shops. Most people have at least one clock in their home and a watch around their wrist.

The Changing Workplace

As towns and cities throughout Europe and the United States grew larger in the seventeenth and eighteenth centuries, the need to track the

The clock on the gateway to the walled portion of the city of Salon, France, was built in the 1600s.

hours and minutes also grew tremendously. Instead of making a living by farming, more people were working in factories, shops, and other businesses in towns and cities. Business owners wanted to know exactly how much work they were getting out of their employees. They wanted the workers to arrive at a certain time, break for lunch at a certain time, and leave at a certain time.

Men work in a clock shop in the mid-1600s. The demand for clocks increased greatly in the seventeenth and eighteenth century.

By the 1900s, more people worked in factories than on farms and most factory workers were required to clock in and out of work.

Clocks helped businesses become more efficient than ever. As inventors provided the world with more precise clocks, business owners were better able to measure the work their employees did. By using time as a way of evaluating each task, the owner could easily see where time was being wasted. An owner could then develop ways of getting certain tasks done more quickly. In time, the assembly line was born.

An assembly line (also called a production line) is a method of building a product in which each person does one specific task. On an assembly line for building cars, for example, one person will add the doors, another will add the windshield, another will add the mirrors, and so on. Workers become very efficient and are able to work quickly because they perform the same task over and over. Clocks made the development of the assembly line possible. They gave business owners the ability to determine precisely how much time it should take a worker to do his task. Of course, this also made it easy for the owner to judge who was producing more or less than expected.

Imagine how many international businesses would be unable to function without keeping track of different times around the world. We live in a global age—an era when one's boundaries extend well beyond the borders of his or her native country. A hundred years ago, very few people in the United States were dealing with people in India or Australia. Now, however, the world has become a community in and of itself—people do business with people in other countries every day. So there is a need to know not only what time it is in your own office, but in the office of the person on the other end of the telephone or computer.

As technology has advanced, so has the need to measure time in smaller increments with greater accuracy. Much of today's equipment needs to be calibrated flawlessly. For instance, a hospital machine that distributes medication on a time schedule has to be accurate so patients are not harmed. Missions into outer space rely heavily on precision timekeeping for navigation. A craft with incorrect timing can drift off course and become lost,

Today, international businesses must keep track of what time it is in countries all over the world.

Astronauts depend on precision timekeeping instruments to navigate in space.

wasting billions of dollars and years of hard work. Military targeting also depends on split-second timing. Timing errors can result in the loss of many innocent lives.

There are a great many reasons why the clock has come to play such a pivotal role in our lives. Let's take a look at some of the inventors who played an important role in the development of timekeeping.

GREAT MINDS AT WORK

Many people have taken part in the development of the clock throughout the centuries. Some of them made huge contributions, others made small ones. But all were important, and without them, the clock would not be what it is today.

The Minute Man

A Dutch astronomer named Tycho Brahe used clocks to help study the movement

The work of Dutch astronomer Tycho Brahe (1546–1601) paved the way for future generations of astronomers.

and positions of the stars. But he was frustrated by the fact that he could not measure time in smaller increments. Up to this point, many clocks had just one hand, the hour hand in 1577. Brahe's contemporary, Jost Burgi, a skilled Swiss horologist, added another hand that would divide each hour into minutes. It was still very inaccurate, but it was an important step in the clock's development.

This globe with a clockwork movement was created by Jost Burgi in about 1580.

Two Men, One Idea

The work of two men will forever be linked in the annals of clock history— Christian Huygens and the legendary Galileo Galilei. Galileo was an Italian physicist and astronomer who led a scientific revolution in the early 1600s.

While Galileo was a student in Pisa, Italy, he took note of the swinging motion

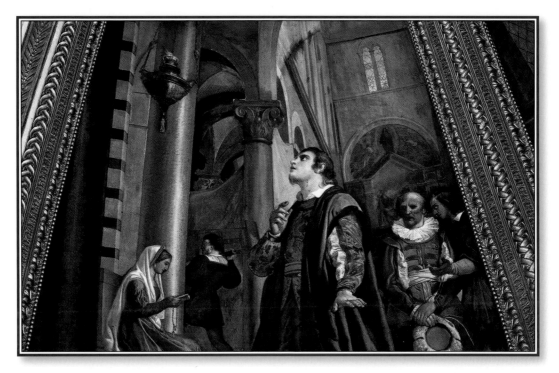

The Pisa Cathedral is home to a fresco showing Galileo observing the movement of a pendulum.

of a lamp during a religious ceremony. He realized that the swinging, also called oscillation, occurred at a regular interval. Knowing that regularity was a problem with clocks, he came up with the idea of applying this motion to a clock's workings, thus creating what became known as a *pendulum.* Sadly, in 1642, Galileo died before he had the chance to turn his ideas into a working clock.

Christian Huygens, the Dutch mathematician and physicist, wanted to improve on Galileo's idea. By 1656, he had figured out a way to make a pendulum properly regulate

Galileo began designing a pendulum clock just before his death in 1642. This model, built in the 1800s, is based on a drawing of Galileo's incomplete design.

clock movement. This, in turn, increased the accuracy of clocks in ways people never imagined possible. All of a sudden, clocks that had been off by fifteen minutes a day were now off by no more than fifteen seconds. Best of all, pendulum clocks required very little maintenance. Their forerunners required frequent adjustments, such as daily winding. Pendulum clocks, on the other hand, could be more or less ignored for days at a time. Many people in the scientific community chastised Huygens for stealing Galileo's idea, despite the fact that Galileo couldn't get the pendulum to work and Huygens did. Many were also intensely jealous of Huygens's ingenuity. Nevertheless, Huygens is remembered for his tremendous accomplishment, and millions of pendulum clocks are still in use today.

And the Winner Is . . . John Harrison

John Harrison was born in the small village of Foulby in northern England in 1693. A bright young man, he loved to work with his hands and he read just about any book he could find. He had a particular interest in the sciences and became a skilled craftsman. Among these crafts was the art of clock making. He built several pendulum clocks, all of which worked quite well.

Then, in 1713, the British Parliament announced it would give a monetary prize to anyone who could produce a clock that

John Harrison won the prize for inventing the first clock that worked on a moving ship. Harrison received part of the prize money in 1763 but didn't receive the rest of the money until 1773.

Harrison's third marine chronometer was completed in 1757.

would work on a moving ship. (A reliable timepiece was needed at sea so ships could determine their exact longitude. The pendulum clock would not suffice because it had to remain still in order for the pendulum to swing properly, and ships were anything but still.)

Harrison took up the challenge and immediately went to work on his first sea clock. It took seven years to construct, and was first tested on a voyage between London, England, and Lisbon, Portugal. Though the results were inconclusive, the ship's captain was impressed and recommended that Harrison continue developing his creation. So Harrison went back to work, investing another three and a half years on a second sea clock. It was much more accurate than the first, but he

The "H5" marine chronometer was completed by John Harrison in 1770 and tested by King George III. It gained only four and a half seconds in ten weeks.

thought he could do better. He used different materials to deal with problems caused by factors such as temperature and friction.

It took him thirteen years to build his third sea clock, and as soon as he was finished with it, he had some new ideas for a fourth that would be much smaller and even more precise. He finished the fourth clock in 1761, and that one did the trick—it was accurate to within seconds. Harrison had made history! He then created a fifth clock— a copy of the fourth—and turned both over to the British government. As a result of his work, oceanic disasters caused by unreliable longitudinal calculations became rare.

Eighteenth-century English craftsmen John Arnold and Thomas Earnshaw have been credited with advancing Harrison's design to increase its accuracy. Arnold's version, for example, was never off by more than three seconds each day. Arnold found a way to decrease friction in the workings of Harrison's clock, which allowed it to run longer without missing beats. But his clocks were also larger (because their inner workings were larger), and they required frequent oiling. Earnshaw, on the other hand, kept his clock smaller and built the workings in a much simpler way. They required no oiling at all. In the end, Earnshaw's design was judged superior and became the model for years to come.

Unfortunately, Arnold and Earnshaw couldn't stand each other. Arnold enjoyed great wealth and privilege. He became friends with King George III, who was a clock enthusiast. Earnshaw came from humble beginnings and

Thomas Earnshaw (1749–1829) was one of the craftsmen who improved on Harrison's design.

Alexander Bain was the first person to create a clock that ran on electricity. This is one of his electric clocks, created in about 1850.

did not seek fame and fortune. The legend says that Arnold, on seeing Earnshaw's superior design, immediately went back to his own workshop, modified it slightly, and then patented it as his own. Earnshaw eventually earned a patent for his design, too, but he never forgave Arnold for what he considered an act of theft.

Time Goes Electric

Scotsman Alexander Bain made the next great improvement in clock design by being the first person to make a clock that runs on electricity. He and Scottish *chronometer* maker John Barwise patented the idea in 1841. The basic premise of Bain's design was to use two clocks. The first had a large magnet on the pendulum bob that reacted to two other magnets placed on either side of it. As a result, the pendulum would swing back and forth. This pendulum was also wrapped with electrified wire, and the regular impulses produced by the swinging were directed into another clock. These impulses drove the hands on the second clock.

Henry Warren built electric clocks that could be manufactured and offered to the public. Born in Boston in 1872, Warren was extremely bright and curious. He loved mechanics and spent hours building things in a workshop his parents set up for him. He attended the Massachusetts Institute of Technology and earned a degree in electrical engineering.

In the early 1900s, Warren and his wife, Edith, purchased a home in nearby Ashland, where he established a workshop in a large red barn. He created and patented more than one hundred inventions there, including an electric clock that was considerably more accurate than Bain's. At this time, some people were beginning to enjoy the benefits of having their homes wired for electricity. Warren built a clock that could run on electrical currents. Unfortunately, the currents sent by early electric companies were unreliable, so Warren's early electric clocks could not keep accurate time. Once a current shut off, the clock would shut off, too. This didn't discourage him, however. By 1916, he had built a clock that could withstand the instability of the current, and in time the electric companies were able to provide better service. Once these flaws were ironed out, his clocks were more accurate than ever.

Lazy or Creative?

Henry Warren had a bright, inventive mind. As a youngster growing up on a farm, he had to feed the chickens every day. He didn't particularly enjoy this chore, especially in the winter when the mornings were cold. So he rigged a bucket filled with feed and attached to a wire that ran back to his nice, warm bedroom. It was also attached to a small, battery-powered mechanism. When it was time to feed the chickens, Henry simply pressed a button, and the bucket emptied, giving the chickens their allotment of food for the day.

Then Time Goes Atomic

In 1945, a physics professor at Columbia University named Isidor Rabi suggested that a clock could keep time through something called atomic magnetic beam resonance. The scientific community had known for years that *atoms* resonate at a regular rate, so it seemed like an excellent idea. Rabi first developed resonance technology in the 1930s as a way of measuring the magnetic properties of atoms and molecules. He won the Nobel Prize in physics for his work.

By 1949, an American scientist, Dr. Harold Lyons, had built the first clock to use atomic resonance technology. It became known as the *atomic clock.* Lyons worked for the U.S. National Bureau of Standards (now known as the *National Institute of Standards and Technology*), which was—and still is—responsible for establishing and confirming standard ways of measuring things such as time, weight, and distance.

Physicist Isidor Rabi was born in Austria in 1898. His family immigrated to the United States the following year. He was awarded the Nobel Prize in physics in 1944.

By the mid-1950s, Lyons and his colleagues had built an atomic clock that exceeded their highest expectations. It was built around the *cesium atom,* which was determined to be the most accurate atom for this purpose, vibrating 9,192,631,770 times every second. This became the international standard for timekeeping. Further refinements have produced a cesium clock that today maintains accuracy within one second every 1.4 million years.

Does this sound like all the accuracy we'll ever need? Perhaps, but it might interest you to know that scientists are working on more refined versions of the atomic clock that they hope will be even better.

The cesium atomic clock developed in 1955 was accurate to 1 second in 300 years.

CHAPTER FOUR

TO BUILD A CLOCK

Designing clocks has never been easy. It has been an ongoing struggle at each stage of the clock's development. In the early years, a time-keeping device was more artistic than practical. It wasn't until the mechanical clock came onto the scene, about the turn of the fourteenth century, that people began thinking of clocks as useful tools.

The Race for Accuracy

Mechanical clocks took the biggest step toward conquering the accuracy issue. Suddenly, clocks were powered from within. The earliest clocks had a very simple setup— free-hanging weights were attached, usually by string, to a cylindrical device called a *shaft.* The string was wound

Many early clocks, such as this one, had only one hand. The time had to be reset each day by comparing the time on the clock to the time on a more accurate device, such as a sundial.

around the shaft so that as the weights fell slowly pulled by gravity, the shaft turned. The shaft was also attached to a set of gears, which would turn as the shaft turned. The gears then turned the hand on the face of the clock. These early clocks didn't have three separate hands for the hour, minute, and second. They had just one hand for the hour. Clocks still weren't accurate enough to measure minutes or seconds.

The problem with this weight-driven clock design was that the weights fell too quickly or too slowly. There had to be some way to regulate the fall. Early clock designers tried a variety of ideas—using weights of differing sizes, enlarging or reducing the size of the gears and the shaft, using chains instead of string—but nothing helped. Then someone (historians are not sure who deserves credit) came up with the idea of adding a feature called an *escapement.* An escapement is a device that steadies a clock's moving parts so the timekeeping is more accurate.

One of the earliest types was called the verge-and-foliot escapement. No one is sure when or where it was invented, but by the mid-1300s, it was being used in tower

An escapement, such as this lever escapement, steadies a clock's moving parts to make it more accurate.

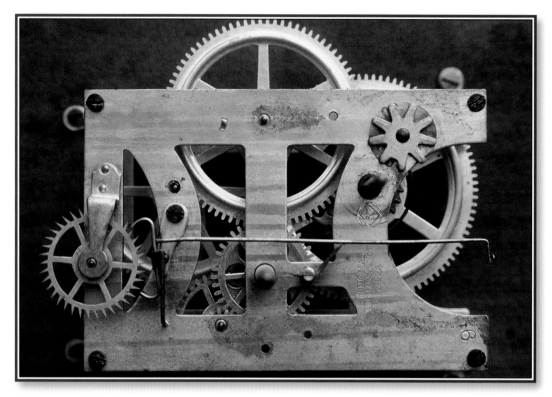

An escapement has parts that go into the teeth of a clock gear to slow it down and regulate the gear's movement.

clocks all over Europe. It featured a T-shaped object. On the vertical part of the T were two small flaps, spaced slightly apart, each pointing in a slightly different direction. These flaps, called pallets, would go into the teeth of a clock gear, slowing it down and regulating the movement of the gear as the T spun back and forth. Weights could be hung on either end of the horizontal part of the T, allowing the user to adjust the degree of regulation.

Another type was called the anchor escapement. This

one didn't come into use until the mid-1600s. It looked a bit like a staple. It was positioned over one of the clock's gears, where it was connected by a pivot and fell back and forth, each side alternately going into one of the gear's teeth. This not only slowed the gear's movement but also regulated the gear's movement to make it steady.

Though escapements improved clock accuracy, the average clock still wasn't particularly reliable. So in the search for greater accuracy, spring-powered clocks were created. The Italian sculptor and architect Filippo Brunelleschi is believed to be one of the first people to use a *mainspring* in a clock. The spring had to be tightly wound so the tension would produce the necessary power. While the spring enabled clockmakers to produce clocks that could be moved around, spring-powered clocks also suffered from accuracy problems. Once again, a regulator of some sort had to be designed.

A little device called a *fusee* became the answer. A fusee is shaped like a cone, and a cord is wrapped around it. The other end of the cord is then attached to the spring. As the spring winds and unwinds, the cord wraps and unwraps around the cone, which rotates. The cord moves up and down the cone during this wrapping-and-upwrapping process. When the cord is at the top of the cone (the narrow part), the leverage is reduced. When it's at the bottom part of the cone (the wide part), the leverage is increased. As a result, the fusee compensates for the inconsistency in tension produced by the spring.

Getting into the Swing of It

A big step toward accuracy came with the introduction of the pendulum. A pendulum is any object that is suspended from a fixed point and swings back and forth due to the force of gravity. For example, a basic pendulum can be made by hanging a ball at the end of a string. In a clock, the pendulum is attached to something called an anchor, which is very much like the staple-shaped escapement mentioned earlier. The two teeth on the anchor move back and forth, each joining with the teeth on one of the clock's gears and regulating that gear's movement. Because a pendulum swings at regular intervals, the accuracy with which it regulates a clock's movement is superb.

The next big advance in clock technology came with

With a single push, an early pendulum could provide correct time within one or two minutes per day (as opposed to fifteen minutes or more, as before). The pendulum was attached to an anchor escapement that regulated the movement of a clock's gears. When the pendulum swung back and forth, the anchor escapement allowed the gears to turn another "tick." Because the pendulum relied on the power of gravity, its swing remained steady for long periods of time.

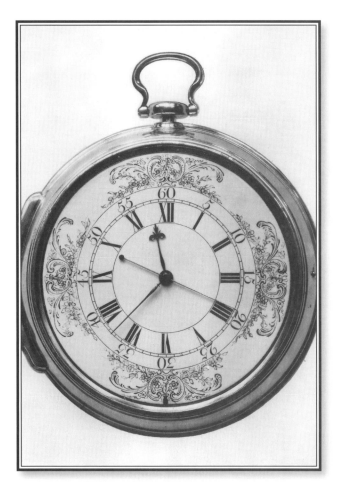

Harrison's fourth marine chronometer was used on a voyage to Jamaica in 1761–1762 and proved to be quite accurate.

John Harrison's creation of the sea clock. Harrison realized that many of the parts used in traditional clocks—such as wood and brass—respond to ambient, or surrounding, temperature and moisture by expanding or contracting. Even though you can't see these changes, they affect a clock's ability to keep accurate time. Harrison compensated for this by using different materials and, in some cases, combining them. He put brass and steel together, for example, because each reacts to temperature in different ways. He speculated that by combining them, he would produce a reliable average. He used gemstones in some of the movement areas because they are less prone to friction and wear. As a result he came up with a timepiece more reliable than any before it.

Flicking the Switch

In the mid-nineteenth century, Alexander Bain came up with the idea of running clocks on electricity. But the technology to keep the flow of electric current steady didn't exist yet. It wasn't until the early 1900s that Bostonian Henry Warren solved this problem. He built a clock that, at least in theory, would run steadily and reliably under electric power. The first of these new clocks ran on batteries. Later, Warren built

Scottish inventor Alexander Bain was born in 1810 and died in 1877.

clocks that could run on the electrical current flowing into people's homes, but he ran into an unexpected problem almost immediately. At the time, electricity was being sent into people's homes with the promise that it came and went at exactly sixty cycles per second. Unfortunately, this wasn't the case. In truth, it varied by up to forty cycles, both over and under.

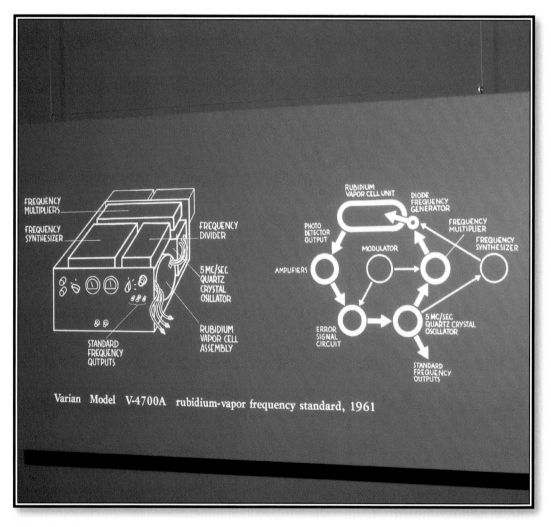

Varian Model V-4700A rubidium-vapor frequency standard, 1961

The development of steady electrical currents made electric clocks very accurate. Soon, however, scientists and inventors came up with an idea for even greater accuracy—the atomic clock.

Warren, along with the General Electric Company, convinced the government that electrical current flowing to people's homes had to be steady. The government eventually agreed and passed laws demanding this. Then Warren's clocks ran properly. Suddenly, all of the traditional clockwork mechanisms were unnecessary. Modern clocks ran on regular electric current, and they were very accurate.

A Tiny Particle, A Huge Idea

Everything in the universe is made up of tiny particles called atoms. They're so tiny that it's impossible to see one without the aid of a very powerful microscope. Atoms move on their own by emitting and absorbing energy known as electromagnetic radiation. This process makes the atoms move about at great speed. This movement—known as resonance—is very regular. The frequency at which an atom resonates almost never changes. When it does, the change is so tiny, it's almost impossible to detect, even with the advanced equipment we have today.

Each type of atom resonates differently, and there are many different types of atoms. When the idea of measuring time using the resonance of an atom was suggested, the first question was, "Which one?" The first atomic clock ever built utilized ammonia atoms.

How We Measure Each Second

The fundamental unit of time is known as the second. Everything time-related is built from this—a minute is 60 seconds, an hour is 3,600 seconds, and so on. But how do we measure the duration of the second?

Today, we do it through measuring the resonance of the cesium atom. Cesium is a soft, silvery metallic element first discovered in Germany in 1860. It melts at room temperature, and tiny quantities of dissolved cesium salts are often added to mineral water. When a cesium atom is superheated and then struck by microwaves of a certain frequency, it goes through a fundamental change in its energy structure. This change produces a pulse that occurs at astonishing speed. When the frequency reaches 9,192,631,770 Hz (hertz), one second has passed. That's right—more than nine billion oscillations in one second! Once this was established as reliable, scientists agreed that this would be the new time standard for the world. Previously, the time standard was based on the rotation of Earth. But because Earth moves faster when it is closer to the sun, this method was unreliable.

HOW CLOCKS HAVE CHANGED OUR WORLD

Today, we take clocks for granted. We're used to them. We can walk into a room with a clock ticking on a wall and barely even notice it. If we're told that we have to be somewhere at a certain time, we simply accept it. We never consider the notion that there once was a time when no clocks existed to help us keep track of time.

The Structuring of Days

Think about it—we get up at a certain time, do our work at a certain time, play at a certain time. So much of our life revolves around schedules and deadlines. Do you want to go see a certain movie? Then you have to know what time it's playing. Do you want to do some shopping? Then you need to know what time the store opens and closes.

There will come a time when you'll have to stop reading this book, perhaps because you have to eat dinner or go to bed.

It's impossible to know how much of an effect time-keeping had on the earliest people who practiced it. There are very few mentions of it in written records. It is safe to assume that an awareness of time gave people from early cultures a more structured daily life. They probably began dividing the days and nights to be more effective in their working habits and so they could have time-related reference points when communicating with each other. If you

A passenger reads the arrival and departure time listings at the airport in Atlanta, Georgia.

wanted someone to visit your home at a certain time, you had to give them some idea of what that time would be—"just after sunset," "at high noon," etc.

Early sundials made these efforts easier because, they allowed the time of day to be referenced by numbers. Water clocks served the same purpose and more. With the help of a water clock, ancient people could limit the amount of time spent on a certain task, such as how long they would wash clothes or feed animals. A laborer could be paid for working a certain amount of time because increments of time could now be measured.

Sundials were the earliest type of timekeeping device. One big problem with sundials is that they don't work unless the sun is out.

A Sign of Success

Clocks had a huge impact on churches and on the many communities that looked to churches for guidance. Public clocks had a profound effect on the early communities in which they were installed. They began appearing all over Europe in the early 1300s and were fairly common by the 1500s.

Clocks were a source of pride, and in some ways also a source of arrogance because having a large clock in the center of one's town or city was a sign of prosperity. Community leaders would work the cost of a clock into their

Many beautiful clock towers can still be found in cities today. This clock is at the Victoria Terminus Train Station in Bombay, India.

taxes, and people would pay them. A new profession also evolved—that of clock maintainer. The presence of a public clock often inspired jealousy and envy in other areas, spurring competitiveness that drove "clockless" settlements to work harder to acquire their own. Some of these towns and cities ran themselves into financial ruin trying to build clocks that were as impressive as those of rival communities.

The clock's usefulness increased with its accuracy. For example, more people were willing to take a chance on the high seas after John Harrison perfected his sea clock in 1761. Sea travel became much safer, and with more vessels bringing more goods to more ports, there was a tremendous increase in international commerce.

Time to Work

Perhaps no other aspect of daily life has been altered by the creation of the clock more than our work habits. Acute awareness of time—down to the very second in some cases—is crucial in almost all facets of business. Once a reliable clock was available, a business owner could measure exactly how long his employees worked, and therefore how much they would be paid. On-the-job efficiency became a topic of great interest. If a worker could accomplish x in one hour, was there a way to accomplish twice that amount of work? This idea was studied

Supervisors use computers to monitor the production of workers in a factory. Accurate timekeeping devices allow employers to figure out exactly who produces the most work in the shortest amount of time.

intensely, and systems for increasing efficiency, such as the assembly line, arose as a result.

When Every Second Counts

Another place in which time awareness is crucial is in sports. Most sports require precision timekeeping. A professional football game, for example, is made up of four fifteen-minute periods called quarters. Hockey has three twenty-minute periods. And hockey penalties are also timed to the second. A player can be put in the penalty box for two minutes and, in such a fast-moving,

Accurate timekeeping is crucial in sports, such as swimming, where a winner is often determined by a fraction of a second.

high-energy game, a lot could happen in those two minutes. In sports such as swimming and horse racing, fractions of a second often make the difference between winning and losing. In these competitions, the whole point is to beat certain times—not only those of your opponents but your own personal best time. These types of timed events would be impossible without accurate time-keeping devices.

A Brief History of the Chronograph

A *chronograph* is a time-keeping device with one purpose, to precisely measure elapsed time. A stopwatch is a kind of chronograph. You can set the hand to zero and then, by pushing a button, start it moving.

The English clock maker George Graham is often considered the creator of the chronograph. About 1720, he built a clock that measured brief periods of time rather than the time of day. In 1862, the Swiss watchmaker Adolphe Nicole built a chronograph with hands could be easily set back to zero. On May 14 of that year, he also received the patent for the chronograph.

In the modern world, timekeeping has worked its way into just about everything. Streetlights, sprinkler systems, and computers all depend on timers. Advertising on television is sold in exact increments, right down to the second.

A stopwatch is a kind of chronograph, a device that determines exactly how much time has elapsed from the time the device is started.

Going Too Far

There are some people who feel we have become too attuned to time. Some people refuse to use an alarm clock to wake them up, feeling that it interrupts their body's natural sleeping rhythms. Many businesses now offer employees the option of "flex-time," which allows the employees to follow a schedule other than the traditional nine-to-five workday, Monday through Friday. Others take this a step further by allowing employees to work from home as long as they accomplish their goals.

This relaxation of strict schedules is probably a healthy thing, as the need to observe every second of every minute of every day is not necessary all that often. Now that we can measure down to the nanosecond (one billionth of a second), do we need to? In some endeavors, yes. But in most cases, no.

Today, many employers allow employees to work from home. This helps many people balance the demands of their personal and professional lives.

CHAPTER SIX

From Giant Obelisks to Tiny Atoms . . . and Beyond

In the beginning there were obelisks—the earliest sundials. They were crude and simple, and all they did was cast shadows that moved with the movement of the sun. But they were a very important first step in the evolution of the clock. They represented an early desire to track time.

Then came the sundial, the kind with a round face and a triangular *gnomon.* Sundials demonstrated an effort to measure time with greater precision by dividing the days into smaller increments. This, too, was a key step in the evolutionary process.

Water clocks arose from the desire to measure time with greater precision, although only in limited incre- ments. The same is true of candle clocks and *sand- glasses.* Then came the earliest mechanical clocks. From

Some watches can be carried in your pocket.

there, clocks evolved relatively quickly and in numerous directions. They were designed in different shapes and sizes and for different purposes.

Watches and Watchmaking

Watches have been around since at least the sixteenth century. Their value is obvious. They can be carried in your pocket or worn around your wrist. They arose from the need to know the time while traveling. Prior to the cre-

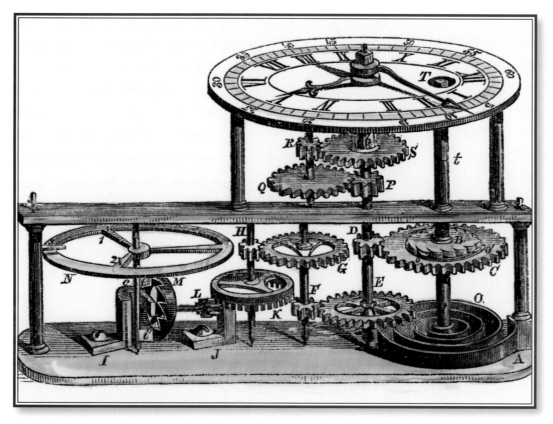

The mainspring is in the lower right corner of this diagram of the inside of a watch from the 1800s.

ation of the watch, some people would take along their household clocks, which were often quite heavy and awkward to carry.

Many historians credit German locksmith Peter Henlein as the maker of the first timepiece intended to be carried. His first watch, produced in the early 1500s, was so imprecise that it was all but useless. It was powered by a mainspring, which wound and unwound with such wild

Pocket watches were often selected more for their decorative value than the accuracy of their timekeeping. Here, a man wears a pocket watch on a chain, or fob.

irregularity that it would lose or gain whole hours over the course of a day.

Early watchmakers, like early clock makers, concentrated on the decorative aspects of watches rather than on their time-keeping accuracy because the watches became showpieces of the wealthy. People didn't want to know the time as much as they wanted others to see they owned a watch. It wasn't until the mid-1600s, when a second spring called a *balance spring* was added, that watches became a fairly reliable tool for determining the time of day. The balance spring helped to control a watch's escapement by making it steadier.

The first watches were worn around the neck or tucked into one's pocket. Then, in the mid 1800s, it became fashionable for women to wear them attached to a leather strap around their wrist. Men generally wore what they considered to be the more masculine pocket watch.

All that changed during World War I. Soldiers quickly realized it was impractical to carry a pocket watch. Many uniforms didn't even have pockets, and the dangling chain of a pocket watch was hazardous. U.S. soldiers who fought overseas noted that European soldiers wore

During World War I, soldiers quickly realized that pocket watches were not practical and could even be a hazard while fighting.

Timex watches were soon available in a wide variety of styles.

wristwatches. It was a perfect solution to their problem, and soon a line of wristwatches for men hit the market.

In 1949, a Norwegian immigrant named Joakim Lehmkuhl who had come to the United States to escape the horrors of World War II, took control of a watchmaking company in Waterbury, Connecticut. He took a long, hard look at the current state of watchmaking and realized

Lehmkuhl created Timex brand wristwatches, such as this model from the 1960s. You can still buy Timex watches today.

he could sell more watches if they were cheaper. He used different materials, improved production, and made sure the new watch line was still attractive enough to draw customers. This new brand of watches was called Timex, and it is still available today.

Technological advancements in wristwatches were made throughout the second half of the twentieth century.

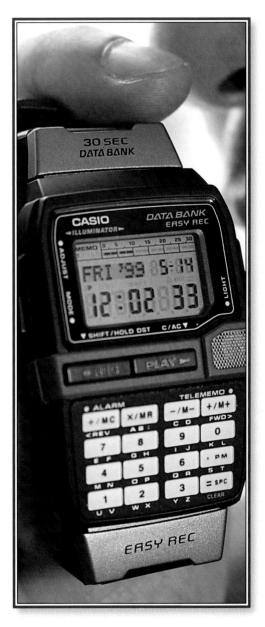

Today's watches don't just tell time. This model has a tiny microphone that allows the user to record a thirty-second voice memo.

By the end of the 1950s, you could buy a watch that was powered by a tiny battery. By the early 1970s, you could get a watch that was regulated by the steady vibrations of the quartz crystal, making watches more accurate than ever. You could get a digital face, which displayed a set of computer-type numbers on a plain screen. Soon watches included the day, month, and year, and some included a tiny calculator. Today, you can do everything on a watch from playing games to taking pictures to sending e-mails. You can spend thousands of dollars on a luxury watch, or just a few bucks on a digital watch that might not be as handsome but still keeps perfect time.

Today and Tomorrow

The future of clocks seems to be heading in the atomic direction. Atomic clocks are the most advanced in clock technology. Our society is as enraptured by atomic clocks as society was enraptured by the first mechanical clocks in the thirteenth century. What is most fascinating about the atomic clock, of course, is its accuracy. It seems as though precision is something we'll never have to worry about again, after centuries of precision being the foremost issue in clock technology.

When the first atomic clock was conceived and designed in the mid-twentieth century, it was the sole property of scientists who worked in large laboratories with lots of high-tech equipment and money to fund their experiments. An atomic clock was not the kind of thing you'd see in the ordinary household. This is no longer the case. Did you know you can go out and buy a clock that will adjust itself, via radio frequency, to one of the government's atomic clocks? You can also download free programs from the Internet that synchronize the clock on your computer with one of these government clocks. Atomic clocks are now also the standard in such devices as the Global Positioning System (GPS), which is a worldwide navigational system provided by a collection of satellites in orbit around Earth. They are also a key component to the many wide-bandwidth communication systems on which our world relies.

NIST

The National Institute of Standards and Technology (NIST) is a government agency with locations in both Maryland and Colorado. Its purpose is to "develop and promote measurement, standards, and technology to enhance productivity, facilitate trade, and improve the quality of life." NIST employs more than three thousand scientists and is at the forefront of the ongoing effort to develop perfect time-keeping devices. Whatever the latest development in time-keeping technology, you can bet NIST is the group behind it. But it's not all they do. They have a hand in many of the things you see and use in your everyday life from VCR tapes to shoes to shampoo bottles. For more information on who they are and what they do, visit their Web site (listed in the To Find Out More section). They even have a page designed specifically for kids.

So what advances in time-keeping technology are likely in the years ahead? The answer may lie in a device called an *optical frequency ruler,* which could be the key to time-keeping devices that are one hundred times more accurate than the atomic clocks that already provide the world standard. Optical rulers are lasers that emit pulses of light that last ten femtoseconds (ten millionths of a billionth of a second). Early experiments suggest that they can better control the frequency of electromagnetic fields, which are crucial in the process that alters the energy structure of cesium atoms. With this kind of time-keeping accuracy, scientists believe they can better understand

and measure many of the fundamental laws of nature. The applications for this knowledge would be almost unlimited. But this technology is still in its developmental stage. Will it become a reality? Only time will tell.

The National Institute for Standards and Technology (NIST) was founded in 1901. Besides helping us keep accurate time, the scientists at NIST make sure that all kinds of measurements are standard throughout the United States.

THE CLOCK: A TIMELINE

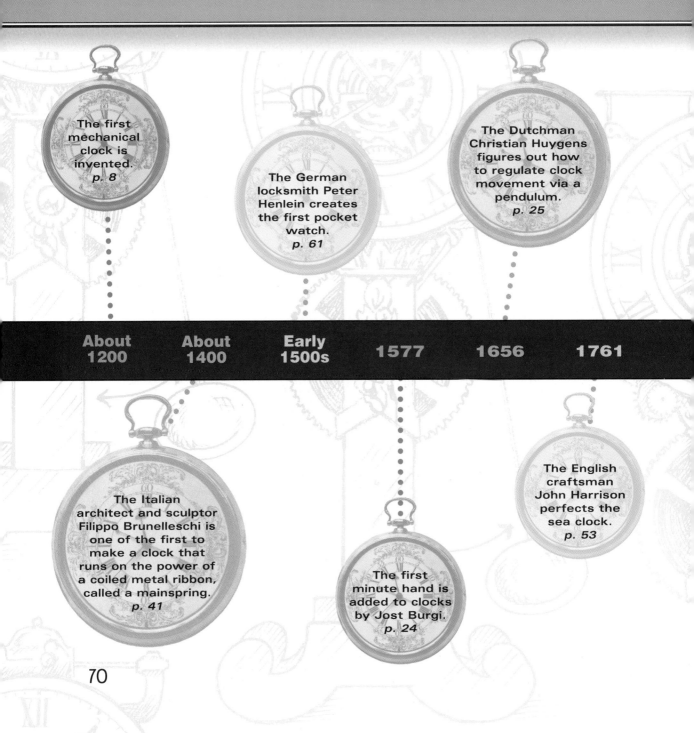

The first mechanical clock is invented.
p. 8

The German locksmith Peter Henlein creates the first pocket watch.
p. 61

The Dutchman Christian Huygens figures out how to regulate clock movement via a pendulum.
p. 25

| About 1200 | About 1400 | Early 1500s | 1577 | 1656 | 1761 |

The Italian architect and sculptor Filippo Brunelleschi is one of the first to make a clock that runs on the power of a coiled metal ribbon, called a mainspring.
p. 41

The first minute hand is added to clocks by Jost Burgi.
p. 24

The English craftsman John Harrison perfects the sea clock.
p. 53

70

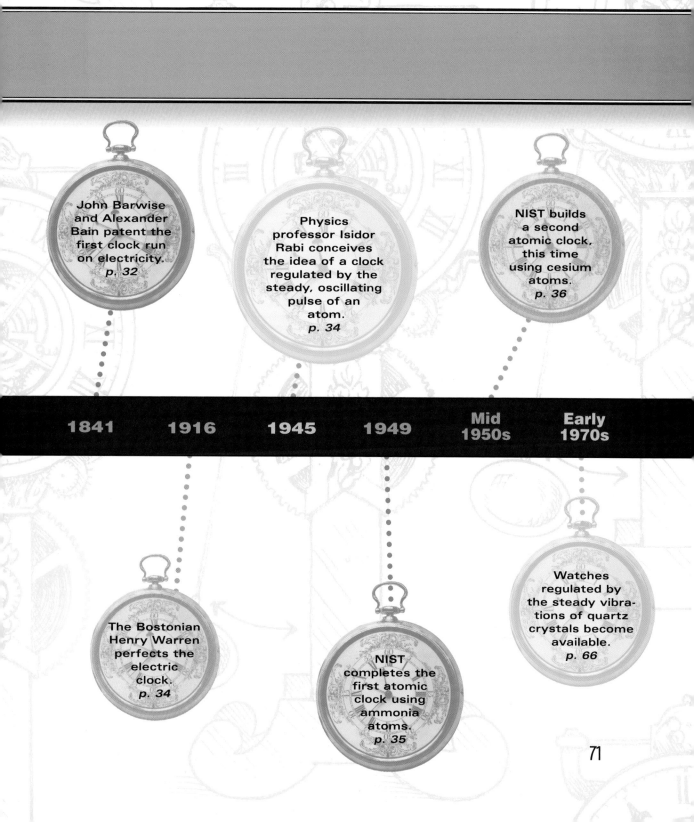

John Barwise and Alexander Bain patent the first clock run on electricity.
p. 32

Physics professor Isidor Rabi conceives the idea of a clock regulated by the steady, oscillating pulse of an atom.
p. 34

NIST builds a second atomic clock, this time using cesium atoms.
p. 36

1841   **1916**   **1945**   **1949**   **Mid 1950s**   **Early 1970s**

The Bostonian Henry Warren perfects the electric clock.
p. 34

NIST completes the first atomic clock using ammonia atoms.
p. 35

Watches regulated by the steady vibrations of quartz crystals become available.
p. 66

71

GLOSSARY

atomic clock: a clock powered by the regular and reliable oscillations of an atom

atoms: the most basic units of matter, microscopic in size and invisible to the naked eye

balance spring: a second spring added to spring-powered clocks to regulate the otherwise unsteady pulse of the mainspring

cesium atom: the atom of choice used to power today's atomic clocks

chronograph: a device designed to measure elapsed time

chronometer: a clock designed to keep very precise time

clock: any device that measures time, specifically dividing days into hours, minutes, seconds, and on

diurnal escapement: the part of a clock designed to regulate the otherwise unsteady movement of the gears

fusee: the small, cone-shaped part of spring-driven clocks that regulated the unsteady movement of the mainspring

gnomon: the triangular and upright part of a sundial

horology: the science of measuring time

mainspring: the central, power-producing spring in any spring-driven clock

mechanical clock: any clock that operates under its own internal power source

National Institute of Standards and Technology (NIST): It is a U.S. government agency that, among other things, maintains and continually develops time standards for the world

obelisk: a tall, four-sided piece of stone that rises to a point and is wider at the base than at the top *optical frequency ruler:* a laser that emits pulses of light that last ten femtoseconds (ten millionths of a billionth of a second)

pendulum: any body suspended from a fixed point that swings freely back and forth

sandglasses: pairs of glass globes connected at a fixed point where sand can run from one globe into the other and thereby measure elapsed time

shaft: the cylindrical part of early clocks around which a string was wound, with weights hanging from each end of the string

sundial: an early time-keeping device that utilized the shadows cast by the sun as it moved across the sky

water clock: an early time-keeping device that was little more than a container with a hole in the bottom that measured elapsed time by how long it took for water to drain out of it

To Find Out More

Books

Borden, Louise. *Sea Clocks: The Story of Longitude.* New York: Margaret K. McElderry, 2004.

Collier, James Lincoln. *Clocks.* New York: Benchmark Books, 2003.

Duffy, Trent. *The Clock.* New York: Atheneum Books, 2000.

Gardner, Robert. *It's About Time! Science Projects: How Long Does It Take?* Berkeley Heights, NJ: Enslow Publishers, 2003.

Levy, Janey. *Keeping Time Through the Ages: The History of Tools Used to Measure Time.* New York: PowerKids Press, 2004.

Older, Jules. *Telling Time.* Watertown, MA: Charlesbridge, 2000.

Somervill, Barbara A. *The History of the Clock.* Chanhassen, MN: The Child's World, 2004.

Williams, Brian. *Measuring Time.* North Mankato, MN: Smart Apple Media, 2002.

Web Sites

Atomic Clock Sync Utility

http://www.worldtimeserver.com/atomic-clock/
A free utility, easy to use and easy to install, that synchronizes the clock on your computer with one of the government's atomic clocks. Allows you to share the most current atomic-clock technology.

Clockworks: From Sundials to the Atomic Second

http://www.britannica.com/clockworks/main2.html
Good general site about the history of timekeeping, presented by Encyclopaedia Brittanica.

How Atomic Clocks Work

http://science.howstuffworks.com/atomic-clock1.htm
An excellent site for learning the basics of the atomic clock. Part of the "How Stuff Works" family of Web pages.

NIST Kids' Site

http://www.nist.gov/public_affairs/kids/kidsmain.htm
NIST's just-for-kids Web site. Games, puzzles, tests, and loads of great information.

INDEX

About the Author

Wil Mara has been writing since the 1980s and has more than seventy books to his credit. Most of his early works were nonfiction titles about animals. In the early 1990s, he turned to fiction. He has since published six novels, a handful of short stories, and numerous early-reader biographies for Scholastic. A lifelong obsession with time and the devices created to measure it (he has at least one clock in every room of his house) led him to write this book. He utilized a variety of reference sources, including countless Internet sites, nine different libraries, and the sound advice from Scholastic's excellent editorial staff.